# All Through the Night

*Night Poems & Lullabies*

*Edited by Marie Heaney*

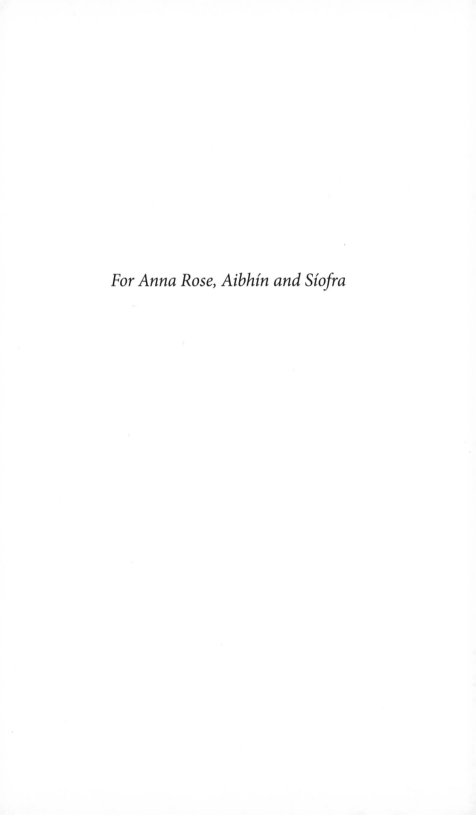

*For Anna Rose, Aibhín and Síofra*

Poetry Ireland Ltd / Éigse Éireann Teo gratefully acknowledges the assistance of The Arts Council / An Chomhairle Ealaíon and The Arts Council of Northern Ireland, and The Doyle Collection.

## THE DOYLE COLLECTION

LONDON • DUBLIN • WASHINGTON DC • CORK • BRISTOL

ISBN: 978-1-902121-61-1

Prepared for publication by:
       Paul Lenehan, Muireann Sheahan,
       Olivia May, Ariana Kaufmann, Daniel
       Tatlow-Devally and Catherine Ward

Design and illustrations ('Titania', 'Alicante', 'Silver', 'Quilt'):
       Paula McGloin, **www.paulamcgloin.com**

First published by Poetry Ireland, 2016, **www.poetryireland.ie**

# CONTENTS

*Introduction*

# All Through The Night

We incline to think of night as a time of peace, rest and relaxation: a time that brings freedom from the cares of the day, a time to dream, to make love and to embrace blessed sleep which, in Shakespeare's words, *knits up the ravell'd sleeve of care*. And this is, indeed, a reality; but night can bring with it other, less benign experiences. With darkness can come sleeplessness and its attendant sadness, anxiety and guilt, emotions that are often more intensely felt at night than during the day with all its distractions. A time when, to borrow a phrase from Keats, conscience burrows like a mole and we are haunted by fears and regrets. Both these aspects of the night, happiness and sadness, are explored by the poems in this collection.

Lullabies, quiet songs to lull a child to sleep and other poems relating to children, form the opening section. The poems in the second part of the collection celebrate the various night-time pleasures as well as giving voice to the anxieties that beset us during the night.

Even in lullabies, there are traces of anxiety. Fears for the wellbeing of the child and the future that lies ahead of it are recurring themes. In 'Connemara Cradle Song', a mother soothes her child but her concern for the safety

*Introduction*

of the child's sea-faring father creeps into the song. Tennyson's song 'Sweet and low' echoes the preoccupations of these lullabies in the folk idiom.

In 'Seoithín Seo Hó', a lullaby in the Irish language, the parent is guarding the child from the Sidhe (known in English as the fairies), who in the folklore tradition were believed to abduct human children and bring them to the world they inhabited, under the lakes and mounds and fairy thorn trees that were scattered over the landscape. And there are the beautiful lines spoken by the fairies from Shakespeare's *A Midsummer Night's Dream* to lull Titania to sleep.

In the Christian lullabies it is angels who are invoked to watch over the sleeping children, though in some of them, notably 'The Castle of Dromore', Christian beliefs and pagan Celtic beliefs are enmeshed.

As any parent will tell you, children do not always respond to the soothing words designed to send them to sleep. This finds expression in the poems written for children, in the voices of children, by Robert Louis Stevenson, a master of this genre. Two of his poems give expression to a child's unwillingness to go to bed. And William Blake's unexpectedly joyful poem 'Nurse's Song' gives happy consent to that wilfulness.

Poems concerning birth and babies might be seen as the domain of mothers, and there *are* poems about this primal

# Introduction

relationship, but I'm happy to include a number of poems, welcoming the newly born, from fathers and grandfathers.

The natural world, its flora and fauna, permeate many of the poems in this collection but it is particularly prevalent in the lullabies and the other poems concerning children. However, I have also included a number of lullabies set in urban environments. Sylvia Plath's 'Alicante Lullaby', a poem full of noise, is a fine example, and there are other poems set in Belfast, Dublin, London and America where local concerns add authenticity and interest to the material.

The poems in the night poems section are very wide-ranging in both emotional expression and subject matter, and they bring the reader to unexpected places. However, unsurprisingly, sleep is still a preoccupation – praise for it, the need for it, the desire for it and the lack of it – and is the subject matter of a number of these poems. The adult's fear of insomnia replaces the child's reluctance to go to sleep. Even Wordsworth, in his gentle poem, 'To Sleep', admits to counting sheep to no avail. Other poets are disturbed by the prospect of the trials that a sleepless night can bring.

However, for some poets even sleeplessness has its rewards: the scent of flowers, intensified by the night air, the birds that are still awake and singing, the beauty of the night sky. The moon comes in for special praise. Walter de la Mare in his famous poem 'Silver' and Ted Hughes in the poem about his daughter, 'Full Moon and Little Frieda', bring the moon to life to great effect.

*Introduction*

Night brings blessings, other than rest and sleep, not least lovemaking, and there are a number of tender, sensual poems by modern poets on that subject. I have included two iconic poems, WH Auden's love poem 'Lullaby' and Sir Thomas Wyatt's 'They Flee From Me Who Sometime Did Me Seek', an angry poem about love betrayed, written in the seventeenth century.

The collection closes with poems that, in Matthew Arnold's words, 'bring the eternal note of sadness in'. There is an elegiac tone to these last poems as the poets mourn the loss of their youth, the death of loved ones, and turn to face, in their characteristic ways, the prospect of that last long sleep that awaits us all.

**Marie Heaney**

**Marie Heaney** was born in County Tyrone and began her teaching career in schools in Northern Ireland. She and her family moved to Dublin, where she still lives, in 1972. She has written *Over Nine Waves* (Faber and Faber, 1994), a book of Irish legends, and *The Names Upon The Harp* (Faber and Faber, 2000), a book of Irish legends for children, with illustrations by PJ Lynch. As an editor with Townhouse Publishing in Dublin she has produced several anthologies, including *Heart Mysteries*, a personal selection of Irish poetry.

*Bill Caddick*

# John O' Dreams

When midnight sings, good people homeward tread
Seek now your blanket and your feather bed
Home is the rover, his journey's over
   Yield up the night-time to old John o' Dreams
   Yield up the night-time to old John o' Dreams.

Across the hills the sun has gone astray
Tomorrow's cares are many dreams away
The stars are flying, your candle's dying
   Yield up the darkness to old John o' Dreams
   Yield up the darkness to old John o' Dreams.

Both man and master in the night are one
All things are equal when the day is done
The prince and the ploughman, the slave and the freeman
   All find their comfort in old John o' Dreams
   All find their comfort in old John o' Dreams.

Now as you sleep the dreams come winging clear
The hawks of morning cannot harm you here
Sleep is your river, flows on forever
   And for your boatman choose old John o' Dreams
   And for your boatman choose old John o' Dreams.

When midnight sings, good people homeward tread
Seek now your blanket and your feather bed
Home is the rover, his journey's over
  Yield up the night-time to old John o' Dreams
  Yield up the night-time to old John o' Dreams.

  Home is the rover, his journey's over
  Yield up the night-time to old John o' Dreams
  Yield up the night-time to old John o' Dreams.

*Thomas Dekker*

# 'Golden Slumbers'

Golden slumbers kiss your eyes,
Smiles awake you when you rise.
Sleep, pretty wantons, do not cry,
And I will sing a lullaby:
Rock them, rock them, lullaby.

Care is heavy, therefore sleep you,
You are care and care must keep you.
Sleep, pretty wantons, do not cry,
And I will sing a lullaby:
Rock them, rock them, lullaby.

from *Patient Grissel*

*John Ceiriog Hughes*

# Ar hyd y nos

Holl amrantau'r sêr ddywedant
   Ar hyd y nos.
Dyma'r ffordd i fro gogoniant
   Ar hyd y nos.
Golau arall yw tywyllwch,
I arddangos gwir brydferthwch,
Teulu'r nefoedd mewn tawelwch
   Ar hyd y nos.

O mor siriol gwena seren
   Ar hyd y nos.
I oleuo'i chwaer ddaearen
   Ar hyd y nos,
Nos yw henaint pan ddaw cystudd,
Ond i harddu dyn a'i hwyrddydd,
Rhown ein golau gwan i'n gilydd,
   Ar hyd y nos.

# All Through the Night

Sleep, my child, and peace attend thee,
    All through the night;
Guardian angels God will send thee,
    All through the night.
Soft the drowsy hours are creeping,
Hill and vale in slumber sleeping,
I my loving vigil keeping,
    All through the night.

While the moon her watch is keeping,
    All through the night;
While the weary world is sleeping,
    All through the night.
O'er thy spirit gently stealing,
Visions of delight revealing,
Breathes a pure and holy feeling,
    All through the night.

A popular version of the Welsh 'Ar hyd y nos',
by **Sir Harold Boulton**

*Eugene Field*

# A Dutch Lullaby

Wynken, Blynken, and Nod one night
   Sailed off in a wooden shoe, –
Sailed on a river of misty light
   Into a sea of dew.
'Where are you going, and what do you wish?'
   The old moon asked the three.
'We have come to fish for the herring-fish
   That live in the beautiful sea;
   Nets of silver and gold have we,'
         Said Wynken,
         Blynken,
         and Nod.

The old moon laughed and sung a song,
   As they rocked in the wooden shoe;
And the wind that sped them all night long
   Ruffled the waves of dew;
The little stars were the herring-fish
   That lived in the beautiful sea.
'Now cast your nets wherever you wish,
   But never afeard are we!'
   So cried the stars to the fishermen three,
         Wynken,
         Blynken,
         and Nod.

All night long their nets they threw
    For the fish in the twinkling foam,
Then down from the sky came the wooden shoe,
    Bringing the fishermen home;
'T was all so pretty a sail, it seemed
    As if it could not be;
And some folk thought 't was a dream they'd dreamed
    Of sailing that beautiful sea;
    But I shall name you the fishermen three:
        Wynken,
        Blynken,
        and Nod.

Wynken and Blynken are two little eyes,
    And Nod is a little head,
And the wooden shoe that sailed the skies
    Is a wee one's trundle-bed;
So shut your eyes while Mother sings
    Of wonderful sights that be,
And you shall see the beautiful things
    As you rock on the misty sea
    Where the old shoe rocked the fishermen three, –
        Wynken,
        Blynken,
        and Nod.

*Irish Traditional*

# Fair Rosa

Fair Rosa was a lovely child
A lovely child, a lovely child
Fair Rosa was a lovely child,
A long time ago.

A wicked fairy cast a spell
Cast a spell, cast a spell
A wicked fairy cast a spell,
A long time ago.

Fair Rosa slept a hundred years
A hundred years, a hundred years
Fair Rosa slept a hundred years,
A long time ago.

The hedges they all grew around
Grew around, grew around
The hedges they all grew around,
A long time ago.

A handsome prince came riding by
Riding by, riding by
A handsome prince came riding by,
A long time ago.

He kissed fair Rosa's lily white hand
Lily white hand, lily white hand
He kissed fair Rosa's lily white hand,
A long time ago.

Fair Rosa will not sleep no more
Sleep no more, sleep no more
Fair Rosa will not sleep no more,
A long time ago.

*Josephine Dodge Daskam Bacon*

# The Sleepy Song

As soon as the fire burns red and low,
And the house upstairs is still,
She sings me a queer little sleepy song,
Of sheep that go over the hill.

The good little sheep run quick and soft,
Their colours are grey and white;
They follow their leader nose to tail,
For they must be home by night.

And one slips over and one comes next,
And one runs after behind,
The grey one's nose at the white one's tail,
The top of the hill they find.

And when they get to the top of the hill,
They quietly slip away;
But one runs over and one comes next –
Their colours are white and grey.

And over they go, and over they go,
And over the top of the hill,
The good little sheep run quick and soft,
And the house upstairs is still.

And one slips over and one comes next,
The good little, grey little sheep!
I watch how the fire burns red and low,
And she says that I fall asleep.

*Irish Traditional*

# My Singing Bird

I have seen the lark soar high at morn
To sing up in the blue,
I have heard the blackbird pipe its song,
The thrush and the linnet too,
But there's none of them can sing so sweet,
My singing bird, as you,
Ah, my singing bird as you.

If I could lure my singing bird
From its own cosy nest,
If I could catch my singing bird
I would warm it on my breast,
And on my heart my singing bird
Would sing itself to rest,
Ah, would sing itself to rest.

And I would climb the high, high tree
And I'd rob the wild bird's nest,
And I'd bring back my singing bird
To the arms that I love the best,
For there's none of them can sing so sweet,
My singing bird, as you,
Ah, my singing bird as you.

*WB Yeats*

# A Cradle Song

The angels are stooping
Above your bed;
They weary of trooping
With the whimpering dead.

God's laughing in Heaven
To see you so good;
The Sailing Seven
Are gay with His mood.

I sigh that kiss you,
For I must own
That I shall miss you
When you have grown.

*Irish Traditional*

# Seoithín, Seo Hó

Seoithín, seo hó, mo stór é, mo leanbh
Mo sheod gan chealg, mo chuid den tsaol mhór
Seoithín, seo hó, is mór é an taitneamh,
Mo stóirín ina leaba ina chodladh gan brón.
A leanbh mo chléibh, go n-éirí do chodladh leat
Séan agus sonas a choíche in do chóir
Tá mise le do thaobh ag guí ort na mbeannacht
Seoithín, a leanbh, ní imeoidh tú leo.

Ar mhullach an tí tá siógaí geala
Faoi chaoin-ré an earraigh ag imirt 's ag spóirt
Is seo iad aniar iad chun glaoch ar mo leanbh
Le mian le é a tharraingt isteach sa lios mór.
A leanbh, a chléibh, go n-éirí do chodladh leat
Séan is sonas a choíche in do chóir
Tá mise le do thaobh ag guí ort na mbeannacht
Seoithín, a leanbh, ní imeoidh tú leo.

Version by **Seosamh Ó hÉanaí**

*Irish Traditional*

# Hushaby, Hush

Hushaby, hush, my child and my treasure,
my guileless jewel, my portion of life;
Hushaby, hush, it's such a great pleasure,
my child in bed sleeping without any care.
My child, my heart, sleep soundly and well;
may good luck and happiness forever be yours;
I'm here at your side praying blessings upon you;
Hushaby, hush, you're not going with them.

On the roof of the house there are bright fairies,
playing and sporting under the gentle rays of the spring moon;
here they come, to call my child out,
wishing to draw him into the fairy mound.
My child, my heart, sleep soundly and well;
may good luck and happiness forever be yours;
I'm here at your side praying blessings upon you;
Hushaby, hush, you're not going with them.

English version by **Joe Heaney**

*Irish Traditional*

# The Castle of Dromore

The October winds lament
Around the castle of Dromore
Yet peace is in her lofty halls
A pháiste gheal a stóir.
Though autumn vines may droop and die
A bud of spring are you.
    Sing hushaby low, lah, loo, lo lan
    Sing hushaby low, lah loo.

Bring no ill wind to hinder us
My helpless babe and me
Dread spirit of the Blackwater
Clan Eoin's wild banshee,
And holy Mary pitying us
In heaven for grace doth sue.
    Sing hushaby low, lah, loo, lo lan
    Sing hushaby low, lah loo.

Take time to thrive my ray of hope
In the garden of Dromore
Take heed young eaglet till your wings
Are feathered fit to soar.
A little rest and then our land
Is full of work to do.
    Sing hushaby low, lah, loo, lo lan
    Sing hushaby low, lah loo.

*Joseph Campbell*

# The Gartan Mother's Lullaby

Sleep, O babe, for the red-bee hums
The silent twilight's fall:
Aoibheall from the Grey Rock comes
To wrap the world in thrall.
  *A leanbhán O*, my child, my joy,
  My love and heart's desire,
  The crickets sing you lullaby
  Beside the dying fire.

Dusk is drawn, and the Green Man's Thorn
Is wreathed in rings of fog:
Siabhra sails his boat till morn
Upon the Starry Bog.
  *A leanbhán O*, the paly moon
  Hath brimmed her cusp in dew,
  And weeps to hear the sad sleep-tune
  I sing, O love, to you.

Faintly, sweetly, the chapel bell
Rings o'er the valley dim:
Tearmann's peasant voices swell
In fragrant evening hymn.
  *A leanbhán O*, the low bell rings
  My little lamb to rest,
  Till night is past and morning sings
  Its music in your breast.

*John Irvine*

# The Winter Night

Wind in the Wicklow hills tonight,
Wind in the hills, and rain;
The doors are closed and the curtain's drawn
And winter's here again.

The leaves are down, the trees are bare,
The streams are wide and deep,
And what's to do for a sleepy head
But go to bed and sleep.

*Delia Murphy*

# Connemara Cradle Song

On wings of the wind, o'er the dark rolling deep,
Angels are coming to watch o'er thy sleep,
Angels are coming to watch over thee,
So list to the wind coming over the sea.

Hear the wind blow, dear, hear the wind blow,
Lean your head over and hear the wind blow.

On winds of the night, may your fury be crossed,
May no one that's dear to our island be lost,
Blow the wind lightly, calm be the foam,
Shine the light brightly and guide them home.

Hear the wind blow, dear, hear the wind blow,
Lean your head over and hear the wind blow.

The Currachs are sailing way out in the blue,
Laden with herrin' of silvery hue,
Silver the herrin' and silver the sea,
And soon they'll be silver for baby and me.

Hear the wind blow, dear, hear the wind blow,
Lean your head over and hear the wind blow.

The Currachs tomorrow will stand on the shore,
And daddy goes sailing, a-sailing no more,
The nets will be drying, the nets heaven blessed,
And safe in my arms, dear, contented he'll rest.

Hear the wind blow, dear, hear the wind blow,
Lean your head over and hear the wind blow.

*Alfred, Lord Tennyson*

# Sweet and low

Sweet and low, sweet and low,
   Wind of the western sea,
Low, low, breathe and blow,
   Wind of the western sea!
Over the rolling waters go,
Come from the dying moon, and blow,
   Blow him again to me;
While my little one, while my pretty one, sleeps.

Sleep and rest, sleep and rest,
   Father will come to thee soon;
Rest, rest, on mother's breast,
   Father will come to thee soon;
Father will come to his babe in the nest,
Silver sails all out of the west
   Under the silver moon:
Sleep, my little one, sleep, my pretty one, sleep.

from *The Princess*

*Padraic Colum*

# A Cradle Song

O, men from the fields!
Come gently within.
Tread softly, softly,
O! men coming in.

Mavourneen is going
From me and from you,
Where Mary will fold him
With mantle of blue!

From reek of the smoke
And cold of the floor,
And the peering of things
Across the half-door.

O, men from the fields!
Soft, softly come through –
Mary puts round him
Her mantle of blue.

*Moira O'Neill*

# Grace for Light

When we were little childer we had a quare wee house,
  Away up in the heather by the head o' Brabla' burn;
The hares we'd see them scootin', an' we'd hear the crowin' grouse,
  An' when we'd all be in at night ye'd not get room to turn.

The youngest two she'd put to bed, their faces to the wall,
  An' the lave of us could sit aroun', just anywhere we might;
Herself 'ud take the rush-dip an' light it for us all,
  An' '*God be thankèd!*' she would say, – '*now we have a light.*'

Then we be to quet the laughin' an' pushin' on the floor,
  An' think of One who called us to come and be forgiven;
Himself 'ud put his pipe down, an' say the good word more,
  '*May the Lamb o' God lead us all to the Light o' Heaven!*'

There' a wheen things that used to be an' now has had their day,
  The nine Glens of Antrim can show ye many a sight;
But not the quare wee house where we lived up Brabla' way,
  Nor a child in all nine Glens that knows the grace for light.

*American Traditional*

# Hush, Little Baby

Hush, little baby, don't say a word,
Papa's gonna buy you a mockingbird.

If that mockingbird won't sing,
Papa's gonna buy you a diamond ring.

If that diamond ring turns brass,
Papa's gonna buy you a looking glass.

If that looking glass gets broke,
Papa's gonna buy you a billy goat.

If that billy goat won't pull,
Papa's gonna buy you a cart and bull.

If that cart and bull turn over,
Papa's gonna buy you a dog named Rover.

If that dog named Rover won't bark,
Papa's gonna buy you a horse and cart.

If that horse and cart fall down,
You'll still be the sweetest little baby in town.

*Stephen Foster*

# Slumber My Darling

Slumber, my darling, thy mother is near,
Guarding thy dreams from all terror and fear,
Sunlight has pass'd and the twilight has gone,
Slumber, my darling, the night's coming on.

Sweet visions attend thy sleep,
Fondest, dearest to me,
While other their revels keep,
I will watch over thee.

Slumber, my darling, the birds are at rest,
The wandering dews by the flow'rs are caressed,
Slumber, my darling, I'll wrap thee up warm,
And pray that the angels will shield thee from harm.

Slumber, my darling, till morn's blushing ray
Brings to the world the glad tidings of day;
Fill the dark void with thy dreamy delight –
Slumber, thy mother will guard thee tonight.

Thy pillow shall sacred be
From all outward alarms;
Thou, thou are the world to me
In thine innocent charms.

Slumber, my darling, the birds are at rest,
The wandering dews by the flow'rs are caressed,
Slumber, my darling, I'll wrap thee up warm,
And pray that the angels will shield thee from harm.

*German Traditional*

# 'Roses Whisper Good Night'

Roses whisper good night 'neath silvery light,
Asleep in the dew they hide from our view.
When the dawn peepeth through God will wake them and you,
When the dawn peepeth through God will wake them and you.

Slumber sweetly my dear for the angels are near,
To watch over you the silent night through.
And to bear you above to the dreamland of love,
And to bear you above to the dreamland of love.

A version of 'Guten Abend, gute Nacht',
sung to the air of Brahms' Lullaby

*Pádraig Pearse*

# Lullaby of a Woman of the Mountain

House, be still, and ye little grey mice,
Lie close tonight in your hidden lairs.

Moths on the window, fold your wings,
Little black chafers, silence your humming.

Plover and curlew, fly not over my house,
Do not speak, wild barnacle, passing over the mountain.

Things of the mountain that wake in the night-time,
Do not stir tonight till the daylight whitens!

*Michael Longley*

# Lullaby
*for Eddie*

The vixen will hear you cry, and the swans
On their eggless experimental nest,
And the insomniac curlew, and the leveret
That leaves a dew-path across the lawn.

*Seamus Heaney*

# Serenades

The Irish nightingale
Is a sedge-warbler,
A little bird with a big voice
Kicking up a racket all night.

Not what you'd expect
From the musical nation.
I haven't even heard one –
Nor an owl, for that matter.

My serenades have been
The broken voice of a crow
In a draught or a dream,
The wheeze of bats

Or the ack-ack
Of the tramp corncrake
Lost in a no-man's-land
Between combines and chemicals.

So fill the bottles, love,
Leave them inside their cots,
And if they do wake us, well,
So would the sedge-warbler.

*Frank Ormsby*

# Helen

*b. 12 August 1994*

The war will soon be over, or so they say.
Five floors below the Friday rush-hour starts.
You're out and breathing. We smile to hear you cry.
Your long fingers curl around our hearts.

The place knows nothing of you and is home.
Indifferent skies look on while August warms
the middle air. We wrap you in your name.
Peace is the way you settle in our arms.

*Paul Muldoon*

# Cradle Song for Asher

When they cut your birth cord yesterday
it was I who drifted away.

Now I hear your name (in Hebrew, 'blest')
as yet another release of ballast

and see, beyond your wicker
gondola, campfires, cities, whole continents flicker.

*Peter Sirr*

# PPS

Welcome 3755547K
your small head rests
in the arms of the state
your fingers are counted, your toes
registered, your cries
have found their way
to a vault of need, you're
known, allowed for, admitted
though mysterious to us
and as yet unpersuaded
you drift and sway
and kick against the world
but listen
your breath moves in a far drawer
a number among numbers
you shift in your folder
you open your eyes
you fall through the letterbox
and climb the stairs
you float towards your basket
and gently surrender
ah 3755547K
recognised, acknowledged, filed,

let the complex systems
convince, sleep
on the miracle of your name
spilling across the screen,
the long arms of the sun reaching in.

Note: Children born in Ireland are given a Personal
Public Service number when their birth is registered

*Vincent Buckley*

# For Brigid

Even in sleep I hear you sing
The husky songs you learnt in school,
And see the widening sunlight bring
You warm as an otter to the pool.

God be praised who gave you these,
The trusting eyes, the burnished hair,
And gives your growing limbs release
In tumbling through the honeyed air.

I praise; and may my praise demand
A quiet place at the end of night,
In which I make your image stand
Fabulous in the cold clear light.

*Eavan Boland*

# Energies

This is my time:
the twilight closing in,
a hissing on the ring,
stove noises, kettle steam
and children's kisses.

But the energy of flowers!
Their faces are so white –
my garden daisies –
they are so tight-fisted,
such economies of light.

In the dusk they have made hay:
in a banked radiance,
in an acreage of brightness
they are misering the day
while mine delays away

in chores left to do:
the soup, the bath, the fire
then bed-time,
up the stairs –
and there, there

the buttery curls,
the light,
the bran fur of the teddy-bear,
the fist like a night-time daisy,
damp and tight.

*Gabriela Mistral*

# Midnight

Delicate, midnight.
I overhear the knots of the rose bush:
the sap pushes rising to the rose.

I hear
the scorched stripes of the regal
tiger: they do not let him sleep.

I hear
somebody's verses,
and they swell in the night
like a sand-dune.

I overhear
my mother sleeping
with two breaths.
(I sleep in her,
my fifth year).

I hear the Rhône descending
and, like a blind father of foam that is blind,
bringing me down.

And after I hear nothing
but that I'm falling
in Arlean walls –
sun-filled.

Translated by **Shirley McClure**

*Sara Berkeley Tolchin*

# Smoke from Oregon Fires

I have driven us out to the farthest parking lot,
close to the cliffs, where my hunger for flight is appeased.
Fall, obediently grey with light rain, hugs the car.
I drift around the shallows of my daughter's sleep;
I would row through it, but she never goes that deep.

When I sit with her in the dark, my arms around
the generous mercies, her childhood memories
are patchworked in the velvet corners of the room,
and round the frog walls streams
the endless ribbon of her nursery rhyme dreams.

She knew she was a girl, knew she would be born
feet first into this silvery world without consent
to decades of continuous sun and decades of snow,
but she couldn't have known her beauty
would be held up to the light and the light would drown in it.

I have her by heart, I recite her, and then she changes
and I'm lost, as if in space, end over end.
Up north of us the firemen are losing ground
to fire; their smoke comes down this far
and smudges out the still October air,

and in our car I'm listening,
and I'm noticing her hair,
the way it's still so fine and fair,
and I am listening to her breathe, and I am
listening to her breathe,
and I am listening to her breathe.

*Gerard Smyth*

# Poem to a Granddaughter
*for Laura*

On the drive from the airport
the road was your lullaby.
We took the straight route, left the detours
for another time.
Tucked in and safe in your backseat nest,
your eyes were closed, you slept
so did not see the garlands of light
the streets were wearing, or the way
the river makes the city two separate places,
parishes showing their age,
traces of the bygone barely remaining;
or the stately edifice where ash once flew
from the burning ledgers of the nation;
the library where I tiptoed among the books
with timeworn covers –
some not read for years, some not read at all,
forgotten like a flip-side song
but waiting for someone like me
to begin at the prologue.
You were passing through
but I am held by the roots to this ground I walk on,
these places I know by name:
all that you saw when you opened your eyes
and looked around
at an old town best seen in the early light of day.

Christmas 2011

*Tony Curtis*

# When I Was a Child

When I was a child
my grandmother told me
that unlike the sun and moon
the North Star never moves.
So what does it do? I asked.
Well, she said, it hangs
around all night like a poet
drinking in the darkness,
making its own light
for the joy of others,
like you and me.

*William Blake*

# Nurse's Song

When the voices of children are heard on the green
And laughing is heard on the hill,
My heart is at rest within my breast
And everything else is still.

'Then come home my children, the sun is gone down
And the dews of night arise;
Come, come, leave off play, and let us away
Till the morning appears in the skies!'

'No, no, let us play, for it is yet day,
And we cannot go to sleep;
Besides, in the sky the little birds fly,
And the hills are all covered with sheep!'

'Well, well, go and play till the light fades away,
And then go home to bed.'
The little ones leaped and shouted and laughed
And all the hills echoéd.

*Robert Louis Stevenson*

# Escape at Bedtime

The lights from the parlour and kitchen shone out
    Through the blinds and the windows and bars;
And high overhead and all moving about,
    There were thousands of millions of stars.
There ne'er were such thousands of leaves on a tree,
    Nor of people in church or the Park,
As the crowds of the stars that looked down upon me,
    And that glittered and winked in the dark.

The Dog, and the Plough, and the Hunter, and all,
    And the star of the sailor, and Mars,
These shone in the sky, and the pail by the wall
    Would be half full of water and stars.
They saw me at last, and they chased me with cries,
    And they soon had me packed into bed;
But the glory kept shining and bright in my eyes,
    And the stars going round in my head.

*Robert Louis Stevenson*

# Bed in Summer

In winter I get up at night
and dress by yellow candle-light.
In summer, quite the other way,
I have to go to bed by day.

I have to go to bed and see
The birds still hopping on the tree,
Or hear the grown-up people's feet
Still going past me in the street.

And does it not seem hard to you,
When all the sky is clear and blue,
And I should like so much to play,
To have to go to bed by day?

*Edna St Vincent Millay*

# Grown-Up

Was it for this I uttered prayers,
And sobbed and cursed and kicked the stairs,
That now, domestic as a plate,
I should retire at half-past eight?

*Irish Traditional*

# Deirín Dé

Deirín dé, deirín dé,
Tá an gabhairín oíche amuigh san bhfraoch.
Deirín dé, deirín dé,
Tá an bonnán donn ag labhairt san bhféith.

Deirín dé, deirín dé,
Gheobhaidh ba siar le héirí an lae,
Deirín dé, deirín dé,
Is raghaidh mo leanbh á bhfeighilt ar féar.

Deirín dé, deirín dé,
Éireoidh gealach is raghaidh grian fé,
Deirín dé, deirín dé,
Tiocfaidh ba aniar le deireadh an lae.

Deirín dé, deirín dé,
Ligfead mo leanbh ag piocadh sméar,
Deirín dé, deirín dé –
Ach codail go sámh go fáinne an lae!

*Irish Traditional*

# The Last Wisp of Smoke

> *Deirín dé, deirín dé*
The nightjar calling from the heather.
> *Deirín dé, deirín dé*
The bittern booms in all sorts of weather.

> *Deirín dé, deirín dé*
Cows go west at dawn's first light.
> *Deirín dé, deirín dé*
My child won't let them out of his sight.

> *Deirín dé, deirín dé*
The moon will rise, the sun go down.
> *Deirín dé, deirín dé*
Cows come home, speckled and brown.

> *Deirín dé, deirín dé*
Blackberries from the bushes peep!
> *Deirín dé, deirín dé*
But first, my darling, go to sleep.

Free translation of 'Deirín Dé' by **Gabriel Rosenstock**

The nonsense refrain *deirín dé* probably had the original meaning of a last wisp of smoke, from a children's game where the players held burning sticks until one of them produced the last wisp of smoke. – *An Duanaire, 1600-1900: Poems of the Dispossessed*

*William Shakespeare*

# 'I know a bank where the wild thyme blows'

I know a bank where the wild thyme blows,
Where oxlips and the nodding violet grows,
Quite over-canopied with luscious woodbine,
With sweet musk-roses and with eglantine:
There sleeps Titania sometime of the night,
Lull'd in these flowers with dances and delight;
And there the snake throws her enamell'd skin,
Weed wide enough to wrap a fairy in ...

Oberon from *A Midsummer Night's Dream*, Act 2, Scene 1

*William Shakespeare*

# 'You spotted snakes with double tongue'

You spotted snakes with double tongue,
Thorny hedgehogs, be not seen;
Newts and blind-worms, do no wrong;
Come not near our fairy queen.

    Philomel, with melody,
    Sing in our sweet lullaby;
    Lulla, lulla, lullaby; lulla, lulla, lullaby!
    Never harm,
    Nor spell nor charm,
    Come our lovely lady nigh;
    So, good night, with lullaby.

Weaving spiders, come not here;
Hence, you long-legg'd spinners, hence!
Beetles, black, approach not near;
Worm nor snail, do no offence.

    Philomel, with melody,
    Sing in our sweet lullaby;
    Lulla, lulla, lullaby; lulla, lulla, lullaby!
    Never harm,
    Nor spell nor charm,
    Come our lovely lady nigh;
    So, good night, with lullaby.

First Fairy and Chorus from *A Midsummer
Night's Dream*, Act 2, Scene 2

*Friedrich Wilhelm Gotter*

# Cradle Song

Sleep little prince and lie still,
Folded the sheep on the hill,
Silent the hum of the bees,
Birds are at rest in the trees,
Quiet and peaceful the room,
Slowly the big silver moon
Rises and peeps o'er the sill,
Sleep little prince and lie still,
Lie still, lie still.

Not even a mouse is astir,
Cupboard and cellar are bare,
Calm lies o'er palace and park,
Never a sound in the dark,
Save for the maiden who cries,
Wakes from her slumber and sighs,
Dreaming as fond lovers will,
Sleep little prince and lie still,
Lie still, lie still.

None is so happy as thou,
Free as a bird on the bough,
Plenty of nice things to eat,
Fine golden shoes for thy feet,
Carriage and horses to ride,

Footmen to run by thy side,
All will be thine if thou wilt
Sleep little prince and lie still,
Lie still, lie still.

English version of the German traditional 'Wiegenleid' /
'Schlafe, mein Prinzchen', from **Friedrich Wilhelm
Gotter**'s play *Esther*

*Nancy Willard*

# Night Song

Farewell child
and farewell lamp

cats that wait
at hearth and hole

farewell mole
and farewell bones

thief at gate
and fire on stones

farewell owl
farewell lark –

farewell dark.

*Sylvia Plath*

# Alicante Lullaby

In Alicante they bowl the barrels
Bumblingly over the nubs of the cobbles
Past the yellow-paella eateries,
Below the ramshackle back-alley balconies,
   While the cocks and hens
   In the roofgardens
Scuttle repose with crowns and cackles.

Kumquat-coloured trolleys ding as they trundle
Passengers under an indigo fizzle
Needling spumily down from the wires:
Alongside the sibilant harbour the lovers
   Hear loudspeakers boom
   From each neon-lit palm
Rumbas and sambas no ear-flaps can muffle.

O Cacophony, goddess of jazz and of quarrels,
Crack-throated mistress of bagpipes and cymbals,
Let be your *con brios*, your *capricciosos*,
*Crescendos, cadenzas, prestos* and *prestissimos*,
   My head on the pillow
   (*Piano, pianissimo*)
Lullayed by susurrous lyres and viols.

*Shane MacGowan*

# Lullaby of London

As I walked down by the riverside
One evening in the spring
Heard a long gone song
From days gone by
Blown in on the great North wind

Though there is no lonesome corncrake's cry
Of sorrow and delight
You can hear the cars
And the shouts from bars
And the laughter and the fights

May the ghosts that howled
Round the house at night
Never keep you from your sleep
May they all sleep tight
Down in hell tonight
Or wherever they may be

As I walked on with a heavy heart
Then a stone danced on the tide
And the song went on
Though the lights were gone
And the North wind gently sighed

And an evening breeze coming from the East
That kissed the riverside
So I pray now, child, that you sleep tonight
When you hear this lullaby

May the wind that blows from haunted graves
Never bring you misery
May the angels bright
Watch you tonight
And keep you while you sleep

*Australian Traditional*

# Yo-Ho, Little Fishy

There's a song in my heart for the one I love best,
And her name it is tattooed all over my chest.

  Yo-ho, little fishy, don't cry, don't cry
  Yo-ho, little fishy, don't cry, don't cry

The ship's under way and the weather is fine,
And the captain's on the deck laying out all the line.

  Yo-ho, little fishy, don't cry, don't cry
  Yo-ho, little fishy, don't cry, don't cry

Little fish, when he's caught, he fights like a bull whale,
And he threshes the water with his long narrow tail.

  Yo-ho, little fishy, don't cry, don't cry
  Yo-ho, little fishy, don't cry, don't cry

There are fish in the sea, there is no doubt about it,
Just as good as the ones that have ever come out of it.

  Yo-ho, little fishy, don't cry, don't cry
  Yo-ho, little fishy, don't cry, don't cry

The crew are asleep, and the ocean's at rest,
And I'm singing this song for the one I love best.

Yo-ho, little fishy, don't cry, don't cry
Yo-ho, little fishy, don't cry, don't cry

*Robert Frost*

# Acquainted with the Night

I have been one acquainted with the night.
I have walked out in rain – and back in rain.
I have outwalked the furthest city light.

I have looked down the saddest city lane.
I have passed by the watchman on his beat
And dropped my eyes, unwilling to explain.

I have stood still and stopped the sound of feet
When far away an interrupted cry
Came over houses from another street,

But not to call me back or say good-bye;
And further still at an unearthly height,
One luminary clock against the sky

Proclaimed the time was neither wrong nor right.
I have been one acquainted with the night.

*Dennis O'Driscoll*

# Nocturne

Time for sleep. Time for a nightcap of grave music,
a dark nocturne, a late quartet, a parting song,
bequeathed by the great dead in perpetuity.

I catch a glance sometimes of my own dead at the window,
those whose traits I share: thin as moths, as matchsticks,
they stare into the haven of the warm room, eyes ablaze.

It is Sunday a lifetime ago. A woman in a now-demolished house
sings *Michael, Row the Boat Ashore* as she sets down the bucket
with its smooth folds of drinking water ...

The steadfast harvest moon out there, entangled in the willow's
stringy hair, directs me home like T'ao Ch'ien: *A caged bird*
*pines for its first forest, a salmon thirsts for its stream.*

*Moya Cannon*

# Night

Coming back from Cloghane
in the sudden frost
of a November night,
I was ambushed
by the river of stars.

Disarmed by lit skies
I had utterly forgotten
this arc of darkness,
this black night
where the frost-hammered stars
were notes thrown from a chanter,
crans of light.

So I wasn't ready
for the dreadful glamour of Orion
as he struck out over Barr Trí gCom
in his belt of stars.

At Gleann na nGealt
his bow of stars
was drawn against my heart.

What could I do?

Rather than drive into a pitch-black ditch
I got out twice,
leaned back against the car
and stared up at our windy, untidy loft
where old people had flung up old junk
they'd thought might come in handy,
ploughs, ladles, bears, lions, a clatter of heroes,
a few heroines, a path for the white cow, a swan
and, low down, almost within reach,
Venus, completely unfazed by the frost.

*Walter de la Mare*

# Silver

Slowly, silently, now the moon
Walks the night in her silver shoon;
This way, and that, she peers, and sees
Silver fruit upon silver trees;
One by one the casements catch
Her beams beneath the silvery thatch;
Couched in his kennel, like a log,
With paws of silver sleeps the dog;
From their shadowy cote the white breasts peep
Of doves in a silver-feathered sleep;
A harvest mouse goes scampering by,
With silver claws, and silver eye;
And moveless fish in the water gleam,
By silver reeds in a silver stream.

*Emily Dickinson*

# 'The moon was but a chin of gold'

The moon was but a chin of gold
    A night or two ago,
And now she turns her perfect face
    Upon the world below.

Her forehead is of amplest blond;
    Her cheek like beryl stone;
Her eye unto the summer dew
    The likest I have known.

Her lips of amber never part;
    But what must be the smile
Upon her friend she could bestow
    Were such her silver will!

And what a privilege to be
    But the remotest star!
For certainly her way might pass
    Beside your twinkling door.

Her bonnet is the firmament,
    The universe her shoe,
The stars the trinkets at her belt,
    Her dimities of blue.

*Ted Hughes*

# Full Moon and Little Frieda

A cool small evening shrunk to a dog bark and the clank of
    a bucket –
And you listening.
A spider's web, tense for the dew's touch.
A pail lifted, still and brimming – mirror
To tempt a first star to a tremor.

Cows are going home in the lane there, looping the hedges
    with their warm wreaths of breath –
A dark river of blood, many boulders,
Balancing unspilled milk.

'Moon!' you cry suddenly, 'Moon! Moon!'

The moon has stepped back like an artist gazing amazed at
    a work

That points at him amazed.

*Samuel Taylor Coleridge*

# 'O sleep! It is a gentle thing'

O sleep! It is a gentle thing,
Beloved from pole to pole!
To Mary Queen the praise be given!
She sent the gentle sleep from Heaven,
That slid into my soul.

from 'The Rime of the Ancient Mariner'

*William Shakespeare*

# 'Methought I heard a voice cry'

Methought I heard a voice cry 'Sleep no more!
Macbeth does murder sleep', the innocent sleep,
Sleep that knits up the ravell'd sleeve of care,
The death of each day's life, sore labour's bath,
Balm of hurt minds, great nature's second course,
Chief nourisher in life's feast ...

Macbeth from *Macbeth*, Act 2, Scene 2

*William Wordsworth*

# To Sleep

A flock of sheep that leisurely pass by,
One after one; the sound of rain, and bees
Murmuring; the fall of rivers, winds and seas,
Smooth fields, white sheets of water, and pure sky;
I have thought of all by turns, and yet do lie
Sleepless! and soon the small birds' melodies
Must hear, first uttered from my orchard trees;
And the first cuckoo's melancholy cry.
Even thus last night, and two nights more, I lay,
And could not win thee, Sleep! by any stealth:
So do not let me wear tonight away:
Without Thee what is all the morning's wealth?
Come, blessed barrier between day and day,
Dear mother of fresh thoughts and joyous health!

*Paul Durcan*

# How I Envy the Homeless Man

How I envy the homeless man
Who sleeps on the pavement under my window
His self-containment, his composure,
His faith in his own fate.

So wholly does he trust in his fate
That when I open my window at 3 a.m.
I am looking down into his face asleep
Like an infant in its cot.

His hands are palm-open to the night sky
Yet like an infant also
His sleeping face fills me with fear,
Fear of his fate.

When I look out again at 10.30 a.m.
I am dismayed to see his nest empty
But then he appears again at the street corner.
His unmistakeable bespectacled figure

Armed with a baguette and a bottle of wine
He climbs back into his cardboard.
Sitting up with bread and wine
He opens a book: *The Da Vinci Code.*

If I had a gram of his integrity,
His courage, his independence,
Even in these last years of my life
I might make a go of it – sing

As I always have yearned to sing
The song of my silence, the song
Of the men and women I love,
Of the places that make me feel at home.

*Máire Mhac an tSaoi*

# '"Ní chodlaím ist oíche"'

'Ní chodlaím ist oíche' –
Beag an rá, ach an bhfionnfar choíche
Ar shúile oscailte
Ualach na hoíche?


'I don't sleep at night' –
An easy boast, but who can measure
The weight of the night
On open eyes?


from 'Ceathrúintí Mháire Ní Ógáin'/ Mary Hogan's
Quatrains', translated by **Patrick Crotty**

*Gerald Dawe*

# Serenade

No end to the strimming,
the APÉ buzzes its way through
winding streets, and under balconies
bright bed sheets rustle like flags.

In the clammy room
not a shred of light, not a bird or voice,
only your steady breathing away
deep down in your own dream world.

The still of evening –
a grey evening, it has to be said –
slates of the house
beyond have loosened,

a slate-grey pigeon luffs by
and from the kitchen
the washing machine's final cycle spins
faster and faster like so many lives.

*John Montague*

# 11 Rue Daguerre

At night, sometimes, when I cannot sleep
I go to the *atelier* door
And smell the earth of the garden.

It exhales softly,
Especially now, approaching springtime,
When tendrils of green are plaited

Across the humus, desperately frail
In their passage against
The dark, unredeemed parcels of earth.

There is white light on the cobblestones
And in the apartment house opposite –
All four floors – silence.

In that stillness – soft but luminously exact,
A chosen light – I notice that
The tips of the lately grafted cherry-tree

Are a firm and lacquered black.

*Seamus Heaney*

# Night Drive

The smells of ordinariness
Were new on the night drive through France:
Rain and hay and woods on the air
Made warm draughts in the open car.

Signposts whitened relentlessly.
Montreuil, Abbeville, Beauvais
Were promised, promised, came and went,
Each place granting its name's fulfilment.

A combine groaning its way late
Bled seeds across its work-light.
A forest fire smouldered out.
One by one small cafés shut.

I thought of you continuously
A thousand miles south where Italy
Laid its loin to France on the darkened sphere.
Your ordinariness was renewed there.

*Seamus Heaney*

# Tiomáint Oíche

Bolaithe na gnáthúlachta
Úrnua a bhí sa tiomáint oíche tríd an bhFrainc:
Báisteach, féar is coillte san aer
Ina séideáin theo sa charr oscailte.

Comharthaí bóthair ag bánú gan taise.
Montreuil, Abbéville, Beauvais
Á ngealladh i dtólamh, tháinig is d'imigh,
Gach áit ag deonú chomhlíonadh a hainme.

Comhbhuainteoir ag cneadadh roimpi go déanach
Ag fuiliú síolta thar a solas oibre trasna.
Chuaigh tine foraoise in éag.
Ceann ar cheann dhún caifí beaga.

Smaoiníos ort gan staonadh
Míle míle ó dheas, áit ar leag an Iodáil
A bléin leis an bhFrainc ar an sféar modartha,
Athbheodh do ghnáthúlachtsa ann.

'Night Drive' translated by **Gabriel Rosenstock**

*Thom Gunn*

# The Night Piece

The fog drifts slowly down the hill
And as I mount gets thicker still,
Closes me in, makes me its own
Like bedclothes on the paving stone.

Here are the last few streets to climb,
Galleries, run through veins of time,
Almost familiar, where I creep
Toward sleep like fog, through fog like sleep.

*Eiléan Ní Chuilleanáin*

# The Copious Dark

She used to love the darkness, how it brought
Closer the presence of flesh, the white arms and breast
Of a stranger in a railway carriage a dim glow –
Or the time when the bus drew up at a woodland corner
And a young black man jumped off, and a shade
Moved among shades to embrace him under the leaves –

Every frame of a lit window, the secrets bared –
Books packed warm on a wall – each blank shining blind,
Each folded hush of shutters without a glimmer,
Even the sucked-sweet tones of neon reflected in rain
In insomniac towns, boulevards where the odd light step
Was a man walking alone: they would all be kept,

Those promises, for people not yet in sight:
Wellsprings she still kept searching for after the night
When every wall turned yellow. Questing she roamed
After the windows she loved, and again they showed
The back rooms of bakeries, the clean engine-rooms and all
The floodlit open yards where a van idled by a wall,

A wall as long as life, as long as work.
                              The blighted
Shuttered doors in the wall are too many to scan –
As many as the horses in the royal stable, as the lighted
Candles in the grand procession? Who can explain
Why the wasps are asleep in the dark in their numbered holes
And the lights shine all night in the hospital corridors?

*Greg Delanty*

# While Reading *Poets in Their Youth*

Reading by candle in the caravan
I'm disturbed by a moth fluttering
around my book and then the flame.
It drops with a waxen, burning smell
that reminds me of Icarus & Daedalus;
how I used to get the two confused
and how I've always wanted to know why
exactly moths are drawn to light;
why starlings batter themselves
at lighthouses and what safeguards
there are for those who fly by night.

*Peter Fallon*

# An Open Fire

He hears the cowherd calling home the cows
and says out loud, Can it be so late?
The boss cow turns her head and flicks
her tail. She has come to an open gate

and she goes in. He is making his way toward
a circle of warmth and welcome, an open fire.
A man full of years. The cows of his life
have herded now to yield in the warm byre.

*Thomas Hardy*

# The Oxen

Christmas Eve, and twelve of the clock.
   'Now they are all on their knees,'
An elder said as we sat in a flock
   By the embers in hearthside ease.

We pictured the meek mild creatures where
   They dwelt in their strawy pen,
Nor did it occur to one of us there
   To doubt they were kneeling then.

So fair a fancy few would weave
   In these years! Yet, I feel,
If someone said on Christmas Eve,
   'Come; see the oxen kneel

'In the lonely barton by yonder coomb
   Our childhood used to know,'
I should go with him in the gloom,
   Hoping it might be so.

*Ciaran Carson*

# Sunset

The street lamps come on
one by one
as an armoured car speeds
into the oncoming dark
the north wind picks up
from lamp post
after lamp post
along the stretch of demarcated road
the union
flags begin to flicker in their tatters.

*William Shakespeare*

# 'Be not afeard; the isle is full of noises'

Be not afeard; the isle is full of noises,
Sounds and sweet airs, that give delight, and hurt not.
Sometimes a thousand twangling instruments
Will hum about mine ears; and sometimes voices,
That, if I then had wak'd after long sleep,
Will make me sleep again: and then, in dreaming,
The clouds methought would open and show riches
Ready to drop upon me; that, when I wak'd
I cried to dream again.

Caliban from *The Tempest*, Act 3, Scene 2

*WH Auden*

# Lullaby

Lay your sleeping head, my love,
Human on my faithless arm;
Time and fevers burn away
Individual beauty from
Thoughtful children, and the grave
Proves the child ephemeral:
But in my arms till break of day
Let the living creature lie,
Mortal, guilty, but to me
The entirely beautiful.

Soul and body have no bounds:
To lovers as they lie upon
Her tolerant enchanted slope
In their ordinary swoon,
Grave the vision Venus sends
Of supernatural sympathy,
Universal love and hope;
While an abstract insight wakes
Among the glaciers and the rocks
The hermit's carnal ecstasy.

Certainty, fidelity
On the stroke of midnight pass
Like vibrations of a bell
And fashionable madmen raise
Their pedantic boring cry:
Every farthing of the cost,
All the dreaded cards foretell,
Shall be paid, but from this night
Not a whisper, not a thought,
Not a kiss nor look be lost.

Beauty, midnight, vision dies;
Let the winds of dawn that blow
Softly round your dreaming head
Such a day of welcome show
Eye and knocking heart may bless,
Find our mortal world enough;
Noons of dryness find you fed
By the involuntary powers,
Nights of insult let you pass
Watched by every human love.

January 1937

*Robert Graves*

# She Tells Her Love
# While Half Asleep

She tells her love while half asleep,
    In the dark hours,
        With half-words whispered low:
As Earth stirs in her winter sleep
    And puts out grass and flowers
        Despite the snow,
        Despite the falling snow.

*Theo Dorgan*

# She Buckles in Her Sleep

Close now, the hurt that has you hurt yourself.

I hear it trickle over the cut edge in your sleep,
The drain of meaning, trust, all that we have
To sing back the dark, the spirit's poverty.

Curl in my arms and sigh, and settle here.
I am no saint or saviour, and I am your grief
Too often, though I would not be.

Shelter, shelter and kindness, this embrace
And this belief: we are nearing the still centre
Where love is again possible, and strange, and rich.

*Maxine Kumin*

# After Love

Afterwards, the compromise.
Bodies resume their boundaries.

These legs, for instance, mine.
Your arms take you back in.

Spoons of our fingers, lips
admit their ownership.

The bedding yawns, a door
blows aimlessly ajar

and overhead, a plane
singsongs, coming down.

Nothing is changed, except
there was a moment when

the wolf, the mongering wolf
who stands outside the self

lay lightly down, and slept.

*Robert Burns*

# Lassie Lie Near Me

Lang hae we parted been,
 Lassie my dearie;
Now we are met again,
 Lassie lie near me.
  Near me, near me,
  Lassie lie near me;
  Lang hast thou lien thy lane,
  Lassie lie near me.

A' that I hae endur'd,
 Lassie, my dearie,
Here in thy arms is cur'd,
 Lassie lie near me.
  Near me, near me,
  Lassie lie near me;
  Lang hast thou lien thy lane,
  Lassie lie near me.

*WS Graham*

# I Leave This At Your Ear

*for Nessie Dunsmuir*

I leave this at your ear for when you wake,
A creature in its abstract cage asleep.
Your dreams blindfold you by the light they make.

The owl called from the naked-woman tree
As I came down by the Kyle farm to hear
Your house silent by the speaking sea.

I have come late but I have come before
Later with slaked steps from stone to stone
To hope to find you listening for the door.

I stand in the ticking room. My dear, I take
A moth kiss from your breath. The shore gulls cry.
I leave this at your ear for when you wake.

*Anne Le Marquand Hartigan*

# The Hawser

*Throwing a Line*

In the deep pause of night
I can think of you
heavy-limbed and lying

turn to me across the ocean
throw out an arm
let its weight fall across me

as a rope from boat to shore.

*Thomas Moore*

# At the Mid Hour of Night

At the mid hour of night, when stars are weeping, I fly
To the lone vale we loved, when life shone warm in thine eye;
And I think oft, if spirits can steal from the regions of air,
To revisit past scenes of delight, thou wilt come to me there,
And tell me our love is remembered, even in the sky.

Then I sing the wild song 'twas once such pleasure to hear!
When our voices commingling breathed, like one, on the ear;
And, as Echo far off through the vale my sad orison rolls,
I think, oh my love! 'tis thy voice from the Kingdom of Souls,
Faintly answering still the notes that once were so dear.

*Matthew Arnold*

# Dover Beach

The sea is calm to-night.
The tide is full, the moon lies fair
Upon the straits; – on the French coast the light
Gleams and is gone; the cliffs of England stand,
Glimmering and vast, out in the tranquil bay.
Come to the window, sweet is the night-air!
Only, from the long line of spray
Where the sea meets the moon-blanch'd land,
Listen! you hear the grating roar
Of pebbles which the waves draw back, and fling,
At their return, up the high strand,
Begin, and cease, and then again begin,
With tremulous cadence slow, and bring
The eternal note of sadness in.

Sophocles long ago
Heard it on the Aegean, and it brought
Into his mind the turbid ebb and flow
Of human misery; we
Find also in the sound a thought,
Hearing it by this distant northern sea.

The Sea of Faith
Was once, too, at the full, and round earth's shore
Lay like the folds of a bright girdle furl'd.
But now I only hear
Its melancholy, long, withdrawing roar,
Retreating, to the breath
Of the night-wind, down the vast edges drear
And naked shingles of the world.

Ah, love, let us be true
To one another! for the world, which seems
To lie before us like a land of dreams,
So various, so beautiful, so new,
Hath really neither joy, nor love, nor light,
Nor certitude, nor peace, nor help for pain;
And we are here as on a darkling plain
Swept with confused alarms of struggle and flight,
Where ignorant armies clash by night.

*Nuala Ní Dhomhnaill*

# Gaineamh Shúraic

A chroí, ná lig dom is mé ag dul a chodladh
titim isteach sa phluais dhorcha.
Tá eagla orm roimh an ngaineamh shúraic,
roimh na cuasa scamhaite amach ag uisce,
áiteanna ina luíonn móin faoin dtalamh.

Thíos ann tá giúis is bogdéil ársa;
tá cnámha na bhFiann 'na luí go sámh ann
a gclaimhte gan mheirg – is cailín báite,
rópa cnáibe ar a muineál tairrice.

Tá sé anois ina lag trá rabharta,
tá gealach lán is tráigh mhór ann,
is anocht nuair a chaithfead mo shúile a dhúnadh
bíodh talamh slán, bíodh gaineamh chruaidh romham.

*Nuala Ní Dhomhnaill*

# Quicksand

My love, don't let me, going to sleep
fall into the dark cave.
I fear the sucking sand
I fear the eager hollows in the water,
places with bogholes underground.

Down there there's ancient wood and bogdeal:
the Fianna's bones are there at rest
with rustless swords – and a drowned girl,
a noose around her neck.

Now there is a weak ebb-tide:
the moon is full, the sea will leave the land
and tonight when I close my eyes
let there be terra firma, let there be hard sand.

'Gaineamh Shúraic' translated by **Michael Hartnett**

*Emily Brontë*

# 'I'm happiest when most away'

I'm happiest when most away
I can bear my soul from its home of clay
On a windy night when the moon is bright
And my eye can wander through worlds of light

When I am not and none beside
Nor earth nor sea nor cloudless sky
But only spirit wandering wide
Through infinite immensity

*Derek Mahon*

# The Dawn Chorus

It is not sleep itself but dreams we miss,
Say the psychologists; and the poets too.
We yearn for that reality in this.

There is another world resides in this,
Amid the muddy fields a pool of blue.
It is not sleep itself but dreams we miss.

If we could once achieve a synthesis
Of the archaic and the entirely new ...
We yearn for that reality in this.

But, wide awake, clear-eyed with cowardice,
The flaming seraphim we find untrue.
It is not sleep itself but dreams we miss.

Listening heartbroken to the dawn chorus,
Clutching the certainty that once we flew,
We yearn for that reality in this.

Awaiting still our metamorphosis,
We hoard the fragments of what once we knew.
It is not sleep itself but dreams we miss.
We yearn for that reality in this.

*Mairéad Donnellan*

# Rock-a-bye

There are nights I need a lullaby,
wish myself innocent,
swaddled under someone's chin,
better still, skin to skin,
ear to a cadence I know by heart.

No matter you don't croon like Elvis,
lose your way in *Love me tender*.
I know we may never reach Babylon,
the mockingbird still has his voice,
so I look to the skies for diamonds.

Under a thrupenny moon,
make this bed a homespun vessel
destined for another hemisphere,
where our sleeping is realised
in dreams we'll leave by morning.

When you do not have the words,
sing me letters, alpha to omega,
held in the crook of your arm,
I'll make something of them,
a lyric to keep me from the edge.

*Paula Meehan*

# The Quilt

It was a simple affair – nine squares
by nine squares, blue on green – spots, stripes, bows –
alternate with gold on red chevrons:
my grandmother's quilt I slept under
the long and winding nights of childhood.

Above the bed a roundy window:
my own full moon. I loved the weathers
wheeling past, the stars, the summer suns;
my aunties' deep breaths, distant thunder.

*Jane Kenyon*

# Let Evening Come

Let the light of late afternoon
shine through chinks in the barn, moving
up the bales as the sun moves down.

Let the cricket take up chafing
as a woman takes up her needles
and her yarn. Let evening come.

Let dew collect on the hoe abandoned
in long grass. Let the stars appear
and the moon disclose her silver horn.

Let the fox go back to its sandy den.
Let the wind die down. Let the shed
go black inside. Let evening come.

To the bottle in the ditch, to the scoop
in the oats, to air in the lung
let evening come.

Let it come, as it will, and don't
be afraid. God does not leave us
comfortless, so let evening come.

*Anonymous*

# Evening Hymn

*Pátraic dixit:*
Tórramat do nóebaingil,
a Chríst meic Dé bí,
ar cotlud, ar cumsanad,
ar lepaid co llí.

May thy holy angels,
O Christ, son of the living God,
tend our sleep, our rest,
our bright bed.

Excerpt with translation from the tenth or eleventh century
lyric 'Tórramat do nóebaingil', also known as 'Evening
Hymn', a text originally ascribed to **Saint Patrick**

*Emily Dickinson*

# 'When night is almost done'

When night is almost done,
And sunrise grows so near
That we can touch the spaces,
It's time to smooth the hair

And get the dimples ready,
And wonder we could care
For that old faded midnight
That frightened but an hour.

*Norman MacCaig*

# Four o'clock blackbird

Just when it was possible to think
the darkness was less dark,
I heard a blackbird thoughtfully
saying what he thought
from a hawthorn tree I'm fond of.
He was slow, but precise. – How lucky
for him not to be restricted, like tits,
to a mechanical rote of notes played
with pianola exactness. And if he didn't have
the acrobatic aplomb of
the wise thrush that says everything twice over,
like Browning,
he was bronze to the thrush's silver
and, between night and day,
made a rich sound that said,
thoughtfully and unhurriedly,
from the heart of a hawthorn tree
I'm more fond of than ever,
that to be between
night and day is to be
between two richnesses and
in a third.

*Theodore Roethke*

# My Papa's Waltz

The whiskey on your breath
Could make a small boy dizzy;
But I hung on like death:
Such waltzing was not easy.

We romped until the pans
Slid from the kitchen shelf;
My mother's countenance
Could not unfrown itself.

The hand that held my wrist
Was battered on one knuckle;
At every step you missed
My right ear scraped a buckle.

You beat time on my head
With a palm caked hard by dirt,
Then waltzed me off to bed
Still clinging to your shirt.

*Louis MacNeice*

# Autobiography

In my childhood trees were green
And there was plenty to be seen.

*Come back early or never come.*

My father made the walls resound,
He wore his collar the wrong way round.

*Come back early or never come.*

My mother wore a yellow dress;
Gently, gently, gentleness.

*Come back early or never come.*

When I was five the black dreams came;
Nothing after was quite the same.

*Come back early or never come.*

The dark was talking to the dead;
The lamp was dark beside my bed.

*Come back early or never come.*

When I woke they did not care;
Nobody, nobody was there.

*Come back early or never come.*

When my silent terror cried,
Nobody, nobody replied.

*Come back early or never come.*

I got up; the chilly sun
Saw me walk away alone.

*Come back early or never come.*

*Lavinia Greenlaw*

# English Lullaby

I have filled the day with dreams
and now must sleep.

It's hard to find the dark when darkness
has no keep.

I live the world too fast, too far,
virtual, residual.

The world is versions, fast and far,
secondary, several.

This island of sky
is filled with signs and arrows.

Each glance in the mirror
opens a window.

I take a pill to cure me
of the speed of light.

I take a drink to fix myself inside
what's left of night.

*Sir Thomas Wyatt*

# 'They flee from me'

They flee from me, that sometime did me seek
    With naked foot stalking in my chamber.
I have seen them gentle, tame, and meek
    That now are wild, and do not remember
    That sometime they put themselves in danger
To take bread at my hand; and now they range
Busily seeking with a continual change.

Thanked be fortune it hath been otherwise
    Twenty times better, but once in special,
In thin array after a pleasant guise,
    When her loose gown from her shoulders did fall,
    And she me caught in her arms long and small,
Therewithal sweetly did me kiss
And softly said, 'Dear heart, how like you this?'

It was no dream, I lay broad waking.
    But all is turned thorough my gentleness,
Into a strange fashion of forsaking;
    And I have leave to go of her goodness,
    And she also to use newfangleness.
But since that I so kindly am served,
I would fain know what she hath deserved.

*John Keats*

# Ode to a Nightingale

### I.

My heart aches, and a drowsy numbness pains
 My sense, as though of hemlock I had drunk,
Or emptied some dull opiate to the drains
 One minute past, and Lethe-wards had sunk.
'Tis not through envy of thy happy lot,
 But being too happy in thine happiness –
  That thou, light-wingéd dryad of the trees,
   In some melodious plot
 Of beechen green, and shadows numberless,
  Singest of summer in full-throated ease.

### II.

Oh, for a draught of vintage that hath been
 Cooled a long age in the deep-delvéd earth,
Tasting of Flora and the country green,
 Dance, and Provençal song, and sunburnt mirth!
Oh for a beaker full of the warm South,
 Full of the true, the blushful Hippocrene,
  With beaded bubbles winking at the brim,
   And purple-stainéd mouth;
 That I might drink, and leave the world unseen,
  And with thee fade away into the forest dim –

III.

Fade far away, dissolve, and quite forget
    What thou among the leaves hast never known,
The weariness, the fever, and the fret
    Here, where men sit and hear each other groan –
Where palsy shakes a few, sad, last, grey hairs,
    Where youth grows pale, and spectre-thin, and dies;
        Where but to think is to be full of sorrow
        And leaden-eyed despairs,
    Where beauty cannot keep her lustrous eyes,
        Or new love pine at them beyond tomorrow.

IV.

Away! Away! For I will fly to thee,
    Not charioted by Bacchus and his pards,
But on the viewless wings of poesy,
    Though the dull brain perplexes and retards.
Already with thee! Tender is the night,
    And haply the Queen-Moon is on her throne,
        Clustered around by all her starry fays;
        But here there is no light,
    Save what from heaven is with the breezes blown
        Through verdurous glooms and winding mossy ways.

V.

I cannot see what flowers are at my feet,
        Nor what soft incense hangs upon the boughs,
But, in embalméd darkness, guess each sweet
        Wherewith the seasonable month endows
The grass, the thicket, and the fruit-tree wild;
        White hawthorn, and the pastoral eglantine;
                Fast fading violets covered up in leaves;
                        And mid-May's eldest child,
        The coming musk-rose, full of dewy wine,
                The murmurous haunt of flies on summer eves.


VI.

Darkling I listen, and, for many a time
        I have been half in love with easeful death,
Called him soft names in many a muséd rhyme,
        To take into the air my quiet breath.
                Now more than ever seems it rich to die,
        To cease upon the midnight with no pain,
                While thou art pouring forth thy soul abroad
                        In such an ecstasy!
        Still wouldst thou sing, and I have ears in vain –
                To thy high requiem become a sod.

VII.

Thou wast not born for death, immortal bird!
    No hungry generations tread thee down;
The voice I hear this passing night was heard
    In ancient days by emperor and clown –
Perhaps the self-same song that found a path
    Through the sad heart of Ruth, when, sick for home,
        She stood in tears amid the alien corn;
        The same that oft-times hath
Charmed magic casements, opening on the foam
    Of perilous seas, in fairy lands forlorn.

VIII.

Forlorn – the very word is like a bell
    To toll me back from thee to my sole self!
Adieu! The fancy cannot cheat so well
    As she is famed to do, deceiving elf!
Adieu! adieu! Thy plaintive anthem fades
    Past the near meadows, over the still stream,
        Up the hillside; and now 'tis buried deep
        In the next valley-glades:
Was it a vision, or a waking dream?
    Fled is that music! Do I wake or sleep?

*George Gordon, Lord Byron*

# We'll go no more a-roving

So we'll go no more a-roving
   So late into the night,
Though the heart be still as loving,
   And the moon be still as bright.

For the sword outwears its sheath,
   And the soul wears out the breast,
And the heart must pause to breathe,
   And love itself have rest.

Though the night was made for loving,
   And the day returns too soon,
Yet we'll go no more a-roving
   By the light of the moon.

*Thomas Moore*

# 'Oft, in the stilly night'

Oft, in the stilly night,
   Ere Slumber's chain has bound me,
Fond Memory brings the light
   Of other days around me;
      The smiles, the tears,
      Of boyhood's years,
   The words of love then spoken;
      The eyes that shone,
      Now dimm'd and gone,
   The cheerful hearts now broken!
Thus, in the stilly night,
   Ere Slumber's chain has bound me,
Sad Memory brings the light
   Of other days around me.

When I remember all
   The friends, so link'd together,
I've seen around me fall,
   Like leaves in wintry weather;
      I feel like one
      Who treads alone
   Some banquet-hall deserted,
      Whose lights are fled,
      Whose garlands dead,
   And all but he departed!

Thus in the stilly night,
    Ere Slumber's chain has bound me,
Sad Memory brings the light
    Of other days around me.

*Dylan Thomas*

# Do not go gentle into that good night

Do not go gentle into that good night,
Old age should burn and rave at close of day;
Rage, rage against the dying of the light.

Though wise men at their end know dark is right,
Because their words had forked no lightning they
Do not go gentle into that good night.

Good men, the last wave by, crying how bright
Their frail deeds might have danced in a green bay,
Rage, rage against the dying of the light.

Wild men who caught and sang the sun in flight,
And learn, too late, they grieved it on its way,
Do not go gentle into that good night.

Grave men, near death, who see with blinding sight
Blind eyes could blaze like meteors and be gay,
Rage, rage against the dying of the light.

And you, my father, there on the sad height,
Curse, bless, me now with your fierce tears, I pray.
Do not go gentle into that good night.
Rage, rage against the dying of the light.

*Alfred, Lord Tennyson*

# Crossing the Bar

Sunset and evening star,
    And one clear call for me!
And may there be no moaning of the bar,
    When I put out to sea,

But such a tide as moving seems asleep,
    Too full for sound and foam,
When that which drew from out the boundless deep
    Turns again home.

Twilight and evening bell,
    And after that the dark!
And may there be no sadness of farewell,
    When I embark;

For tho' from out our bourne of Time and Place
    The flood may bear me far,
I hope to see my Pilot face to face
    When I have crost the bar.

*William Shakespeare*

# 'Now cracks a noble heart'

Now cracks a noble heart.
Good night, sweet prince:
And flights of angels sing thee to thy rest!

Horatio from *Hamlet*, Act 5 Scene 2

# Acknowledgements

JOHN O' DREAMS by **Bill Caddick**, with kind permission of the author.

AR HYD Y NOS, courtesy of Draig Werdd: the Welsh Society in Ireland.

A DUTCH LULLABY by **Eugene Field**, from *More Favourite Poems We Learned in School* (Mercier Press, 1994), edited by Thomas F Walsh.

A CRADLE SONG by **WB Yeats**, from *The Poems* (JM Dent, 1994, Everyman edition), edited by Daniel Albright.

SEOITHÍN, SEO HÓ, Irish traditional. Irish version and English translation by **Seosamh Ó hÉanaí / Joe Heaney**.

THE GARTAN MOTHER'S LULLABY by **Joseph Campbell**, from *The Poems of Joseph Campbell* (Allen Figgis, 1963), edited by Austin Clarke.

THE WINTER NIGHT by **John Irvine**, from *Moon Cradle: Lullabies and Dandling Songs from Ireland with Old Childhood Favourites* (O'Brien Press, 1991), with kind permission of Pat Donlon and Maddy Glas.

CONNEMARA CRADLE SONG, lyrics by **Delia Murphy**, with kind permission of White Hound Music.

SWEET AND LOW by **Alfred, Lord Tennyson**, from *The Princess* (Macmillan and Company).

A CRADLE SONG by **Padraic Colum**, from *Collected Poems* (Devin-Adair, 1953), by kind permission of the Estate of Padraic Colum.

GRACE FOR LIGHT by **Moira O'Neill**, from *Songs of the Glens of Antrim* (1900).

HUSH, LITTLE BABY, American traditional, from *Moon Cradle: Lullabies and Dandling Songs from Ireland with Old Childhood Favourites* (O'Brien Press, 1991), with kind permission of Pat Donlon and Maddy Glas.

LULLABY OF A WOMAN OF THE MOUNTAIN by **Pádraig Pearse**, from *The 1916 Poets* (Gill and Macmillan, 1995), edited by Desmond Ryan.

LULLABY by **Michael Longley**, from *A Hundred Doors* (2011), with kind permission of the author and Penguin Random House UK, 80 Strand, London.

SERENADES by **Seamus Heaney**, from *Opened Ground: Poems 1966-1996* (1998), with kind permission of the author's Estate and Faber and Faber, Bloomsbury House, 74-77 Great Russell Street, London.

HELEN by **Frank Ormsby**, from *Goat's Milk: New and Selected Poems* (2015), with kind permission of the author and Bloodaxe Books, Eastburn, South Park, Hexham, Northumberland.

CRADLE SONG FOR ASHER by **Paul Muldoon**, from *Moy Sand and Gravel* (2002), with kind permission of the author and Faber and Faber, Bloomsbury House, 74-77 Great Russell Street, London.

PPS by **Peter Sirr**, from *The Thing Is* (2009), with kind permission of the author and The Gallery Press, Loughcrew, Oldcastle, Co Meath.

FOR BRIGID by **Vincent Buckley**, from *Last Poems* (1991), with kind permission of Penguin Random House Australia, 707 Collins Street, Melbourne.

ENERGIES by **Eavan Boland**, from *New Collected Poems* (2005), with kind permission of the author and Carcanet Press, 4th Floor, Alliance House, 30 Cross Street, Manchester.

MIDNIGHT by **Gabriela Mistral**, from *Poetry Ireland Review* 18/19 (ed. by Ciarán Cosgrove), with kind permission of **Shirley McClure**.

SMOKE FROM OREGON FIRES by **Sara Berkeley Tolchin**, from *Strawberry Thief* (2005), with kind permission of the author and The Gallery Press, Loughcrew, Oldcastle, Co Meath.

POEM TO A GRANDDAUGHTER by **Gerard Smyth**, from *A Song of Elsewhere* (2015), with kind permission of the author and Dedalus Press, 13 Moyclare Road, Baldoyle, Dublin.

WHEN I WAS A CHILD by **Tony Curtis**, from *Approximately in the Key of C* (2015), with kind permission of the author and Arc Publications, Nanholme Mill, Shaw Wood Road, Todmorden, Lancashire.

NURSE'S SONG by **William Blake**, from *The New Penguin Book of Romantic Poetry* (2001), edited by Jonathan and Jessica Wordsworth.

ESCAPE AT BEDTIME by **Robert Louis Stevenson**, from *Poems: A Child's Garden of Verses, Underwoods, Songs of Travel* (Thomas Nelson and Sons).

BED IN SUMMER by **Robert Louis Stevenson**, from *Poems: A Child's Garden of Verses, Underwoods, Songs of Travel* (Thomas Nelson and Sons).

GROWN-UP by **Edna St Vincent Millay**, from *Collected Poems* (Harper and Row). Copyright 1923, 1951, by Edna St Vincent Millay and Norma Millay Ellis. Reprinted with the permission of Holly Peppe, Literary Executor, The Millay Society, **www.millay.org**.

DEIRÍN DÉ, Irish traditional. English version, THE LAST WISP OF SMOKE, with kind permission of **Gabriel Rosenstock**.

NIGHT SONG by **Nancy Willard**, from *Water Walker* (Alfred A Knopf, 1989), with kind permission of the author and the Jean V Naggar Literary Agency, 216 E. 75th Street, Suite 1E, New York.

ALICANTE LULLABY by **Sylvia Plath**, from *Collected Poems* (1981), with kind permission of Faber and Faber, Bloomsbury House, 74-77 Great Russell Street, London.

LULLABY OF LONDON, words and music by **Shane MacGowan**, © 1988 Universal Music Publishing Limited. All Rights Reserved.

NÍ CHODLAÍM IST OÍCHE by **Máire Mhac an tSaoi** from *Margadh Na Saoire* (Sáirséal agus Dill, 1956) with kind permission of the author. English translation, I DON'T SLEEP AT NIGHT, from *The Penguin Book of Irish Poetry* (2010), with kind permission of **Patrick Crotty.**

SERENADE by **Gerald Dawe**, from *Mickey Finn's Air* (2014), with kind permission of the author and The Gallery Press, Loughcrew, Oldcastle, Co Meath.

11 RUE DAGUERRE by **John Montague**, from *New Collected Poems* (2012), with kind permission of the author and The Gallery Press, Loughcrew, Oldcastle, Co Meath.

NIGHT DRIVE by **Seamus Heaney**, from *Door into the Dark* (1969), with kind permission of the author's Estate and Faber and Faber, Bloomsbury House, 74-77 Great Russell Street, London. Irish translation, TIOMÁINT OÍCHE from *Conlán* (1989), with kind permission of **Gabriel Rosenstock** and Coiscéim, Tig Bhríde, 91 Bóthar Bhinn Éadair, Binn Éadair, Baile Átha Cliath 13.

THE NIGHT PIECE by **Thom Gunn**, from *Collected Poems* (1995), with kind permission of Faber and Faber, Bloomsbury House, 74-77 Great Russell Street, London.

THE COPIOUS DARK by **Eiléan Ní Chuilleanáin**, from *The Sun-Fish* (2009), with kind permission of the author and The Gallery Press, Loughcrew, Oldcastle, Co Meath.

WHILE READING *POETS IN THEIR YOUTH* by **Greg Delanty**, from *Collected Poems 1986-2006* (2006), with kind permission of the author and Carcanet Press, 4th Floor, Alliance House, 30 Cross Street, Manchester.

AN OPEN FIRE by **Peter Fallon**, from *News of the World* (1998), with kind permission of the author and The Gallery Press, Loughcrew, Oldcastle, Co Meath.

THE OXEN by **Thomas Hardy**, from *Thomas Hardy: Poems Selected by Tom Paulin* (Faber and Faber, 2001).

SUNSET by **Ciaran Carson**, from *From Elsewhere* (2014), with kind permission of the author and The Gallery Press, Loughcrew, Oldcastle, Co Meath.

LULLABY by **WH Auden**, from *Collected Poems* (Faber and Faber, 2007), with kind permission of the Estate of WH Auden.

SHE TELLS HER LOVE WHILE HALF ASLEEP by **Robert Graves**, from *Complete Poems* (2000), with kind permission of Carcanet Press, 4th Floor, Alliance House, 30 Cross Street, Manchester.

SHE BUCKLES IN HER SLEEP by **Theo Dorgan**, from *What This Earth Cost Us* (2008), with kind permission of the author and Dedalus Press, 13 Moyclare Road, Baldoyle, Dublin.

AFTER LOVE by **Maxine Kumin**, from *Selected Poems, 1960-1990* (1997), with kind permission of WW Norton and Company, 500 Fifth Avenue, New York.

LASSIE LIE NEAR ME by **Robert Burns**, from *Selected Poems* (Penguin Classics, 1993), edited by Carol McGuirk.

I LEAVE THIS AT YOUR EAR by **WS Graham**, from *Collected Poems: 1942-1977* (Faber and Faber, 1979), with kind permission of Rosalind Mudaliar.

THE HAWSER by **Anne Le Marquand Hartigan**, from *To Keep the Light Burning: Reflections in Times of Loss* (2008), with kind permission of the author and Salmon Poetry, Knockeven, Cliffs of Moher, Co Clare.

AT THE MID HOUR OF NIGHT by **Thomas Moore**, from *Irish Melodies* (1865).

DOVER BEACH by **Matthew Arnold**, from *The Faber Book of Landscape Poetry* (2000), edited by Geoffrey Grigson.

GAINEAMH SHÚRAIC by **Nuala Ní Dhomhnaill**, from *Féar Suaithinseach* (An Sagart, 1984), with kind permission of the author. English translation, QUICKSAND, with kind permission of the Estate of **Michael Hartnett**, c/o The Gallery Press, Loughcrew, Oldcastle, Co Meath.

I'M HAPPIEST WHEN MOST AWAY by **Emily Brontë**, from *Emily Jane Brontë: The Complete Poems* (Penguin Books, 1992), edited by Janet Gezari.

THE DAWN CHORUS by **Derek Mahon**, from *New Collected Poems* (2011), with kind permission of the author and The Gallery Press, Loughcrew, Oldcastle, Co Meath.

ROCK-A-BYE by **Mairéad Donnellan**, from *Under a Thrupenny Moon* (Litlab, 2013), with kind permission of the author.

THE QUILT by **Paula Meehan**, from *Geomantic* (2016), with kind permission of the author and Dedalus Press, 13 Moyclare Road, Baldoyle, Dublin.

LET EVENING COME by **Jane Kenyon**, from *Collected Poems* (2005), copyright the Estate of Jane Kenyon, reprinted with the permission of The Permissions Company, Inc., on behalf of Graywolf Press.

EVENING HYMN, from *Early Irish lyrics, eighth to twelfth century* (Clarendon Press, 1956), edited by Gerard Murphy.

WHEN NIGHT IS ALMOST DONE by **Emily Dickinson**, from *The Works of Emily Dickinson* (Wordsworth Editions, 1994).

FOUR O'CLOCK BLACKBIRD by **Norman MacCaig**, from *The Poems of Norman MacCaig* (2009), with kind permission of the author's Estate and Birlinn Ltd / Polygon, West Newington House, 10 Newington Rd, Edinburgh.

MY PAPA'S WALTZ by Theodore Roethke from *Collected Poems* (1985), with kind permission of Faber and Faber, Bloomsbury House, 74-77 Great Russell Street, London.

AUTOBIOGRAPHY by Louis MacNeice, from *Collected Poems* (Faber and Faber, 1966), with kind permission of David Higham Associates, 7th Floor, Waverley House, 7-12 Noel Street, London.

ENGLISH LULLABY by Lavinia Greenlaw, from *From the Casual Perfect* (2011), with kind permission of the author and Faber and Faber, Bloomsbury House, 74-77 Great Russell Street, London.

THEY FLEE FROM ME by Sir Thomas Wyatt, from *The Norton Anthology of English Literature: Volume 1*, 8th edition (WW Norton and Company, 2006), Stephen Greenblatt (General Editor).

ODE TO A NIGHTINGALE by John Keats, from *The New Penguin Book of Romantic Poetry* (2001), edited by Jonathan and Jessica Wordsworth.

WE'LL GO NO MORE A-ROVING by George Gordon, Lord Byron, from *The New Penguin Book of Romantic Poetry* (2001), edited by Jonathan and Jessica Wordsworth.

OFT, IN THE STILLY NIGHT by Thomas Moore, from *The Poetical Works of Thomas Moore Including His Melodies, Ballads, Etc.*, (A and W Galignani, 1829).

DO NOT GO GENTLE INTO THAT GOOD NIGHT by Dylan Thomas, from *Collected Poems 1934-1952* (JM Dent, 1952), with kind permission of David Higham Associates, 7th Floor, Waverley House, 7-12 Noel Street, London.

CROSSING THE BAR by Alfred, Lord Tennyson, from *Alfred, Lord Tennyson* (JM Dent, 1996, Everyman edition), edited by Michael Baron.

With Special Thanks To:

**Treasa Coady, Anne Devlin,
Polly Devlin, Catherine Heaney**
and **Niall MacMonagle**